Adapting Your Business
Navigating the Path to a Sustainable Future

Table of Contents

Chapter 1. Introduction

In today's rapidly evolving business landscape, foresight, resilience, and adaptability are the ingredients of success. Our latest Special Report, "Adapting Your Business: Navigating the Path to a Sustainable Future," aims to be your lighthouse in these turbulent times. This engaging, comprehensive, and practical guide is far from your typical heavy business analysis. Instead, it's an exhilarating roadmap that lays the steppingstones for building a future-proof business, focusing on sustainability and enduring growth. It's packed with case studies, expert insights, and innovative strategies designed to propel your business forward. Reading it will feel akin to finding a treasure map that points to an unclaimed island of opportunities, heightened profitability, and long-term sustainability. Come join us on this journey and let's turn your enterprise into a beacon of adaptability in the changing tides of the business world!

Chapter 2. Understanding Sustainability in a Business Context

Nestled at the heart of any future-proof business, sustainability represents a holistic approach that marries environmental responsibility, social equity, and economic viability – the enduring triad forming the cornerstone of sustainable decisions, strategies, and practices.

It is crucial to dissect the concept of sustainability, particularly within a business context, in order to fully grasp its nuances, significance, and potential. In depth, we will be examining its three pivotal spheres: the environmental aspect, the social aspect, and the economic aspect, along with strategies to incorporate sustainability in your business model.

2.1. The Environmental Aspect of Sustainability

This aspect focuses on minimizing business-related environmental damage. Sustainable businesses strive to decrease their carbon footprints, conserve resources, encourage biodiversity, and limit waste production.

For instance, Interface, a carpet tile manufacturer, has worked relentlessly to minimize its environmental impact by adopting environmentally-friendly methods, like recycling flimsy fishing nets into durable carpet fibers. Such innovative and eco-friendly approach not only reduced harmful oceanic waste but also underscored Interface's commitment to ecological security.

2.2. The Social Aspect of Sustainability

The social aspect is equally invaluable, emphasizing the importance of maintaining equitable societies. It encapsulates fair treatment, labor practices, employee rights, community development, health and safety, and human rights.

A shining example is The Body Shop, which has vested a keen interest in fair trade practices. It fosters ethical sourcing, contributing to a more equitable world by ensuring that its trade agreements uphold and protect communities involved in their supply chain.

2.3. The Economic Aspect of Sustainability

The economic aspect focuses on engendering economic strength and resilience to enable a company to thrive over time. Central to this is efficiency, risk management, and adhering to the principles of circular economy.

Unilever's 'Sustainable Living' plan that sought to harmonize long-term growth with sustainability is a good example. The company has taken steps to leverage sustainability as a pathway to expedite growth, reducing waste and costs while boosting resilience to fluctuating resources prices.

2.4. Implementing Sustainability in a Business Model

Incorporating sustainability into a business model can be achieved in myriad ways and must be tailored according to a company's size, industry, customer base, resources, and culture.

One route to do so is by optimizing operations, minimizing waste, and embracing technologies that curb environmental impact. Firms can resort to 'green' procurement policies, prioritizing the purchase of environmentally friendly, ethically sourced, and energy-efficient items.

2.5. The Role of Leadership

Leadership plays a vital role in sustainability-driven transformation. Leaders need to communicate the rationale behind this shift and demonstrate commitment through their actions. They should encourage employees to adopt sustainable practices and instill this mindset in all aspects of the business.

2.6. Embracing Sustainable Innovation

Businesses should look to drive sustainable innovation, taking 'green' ideas from ideation to fruition. Whether it's through new products or refining existing offerings, sustainable innovation can help businesses differentiate themselves and gain a competitive edge.

2.7. Measuring Sustainability

Sustainability, similar to other corporate objectives, must be measured and managed. Tools like Global Reporting Initiative (GRI) standards, Carbon Disclosure Project (CDP), B Corporations, and Circularity Indicators can be used to assess and continually improve a company's sustainability performance.

2.8. The Power of Collaboration

Businesses don't have to navigate the path to sustainability alone. Collaboration with stakeholders, NGOs, and even competitors can accelerate the shift to more sustainable operations.

Remember, sustainability is no longer optional; it's a business imperative in this rapidly evolving landscape. Businesses that embrace this reality and intertwine sustainability into their DNA will not only survive but also thrive. As we elucidate ways to embed sustainability more concretely in business conduct, let the thread of sustainable thought weave itself into your perspectives, strategies, and operations, shaping your business to resonate strongly with the sustainability agenda. Only then can we envisage a business future that is vibrant and sustainable.

Chapter 3. Fostering a Culture of Adaptability and Innovation

The capacity to adapt, to anticipate and respond to changes, is the distinctive trait of a thriving business. Regardless of the scale or industry, companies must continually evolve to address the shifting needs of their customers, the increasing complexities of the marketplace and the relentless pace of technological advancement. This adaptability, however, isn't a characteristic that naturally occurs or is brought by the tides of time. It requires a concerted effort to cultivate a corporate culture that values and promotes it. Similarly, innovation is not a luxury or a choice, but rather the lifeblood of a company aspiring to survive and thrive in the evolving global business landscape.

3.1. Fostering an Inclusive Mindset

Companies often misconstrue adaptability as merely being amenable to change. It is, however, far more than that. It is about creating an inclusive mindset that underscores the importance of every team member in driving change. Proactive behaviors must be encouraged at all levels, from the frontline staff up to the senior executives. Individuals should feel empowered to challenge the status quo and voice their ideas, without the fear of retaliation or scorn. An open dialogue lays the foundation for an environment of trust, a critical element in driving adaptability and innovation.

3.2. Encouraging Experimentation

To galvanize innovation, a business must not only tolerate but also encourage, the art of experimentation. The understanding that mistakes are stepping stones to success and not roadblocks must infiltrate the business at all levels. Although a failed experiment may seem like a drain on resources initially, these "controlled failures" can lead to exponential gains in the future. The learning outcomes of the so-called 'failures' are the lessons that can be integrated into future plans and strategies.

3.3. Emphasizing Continuous Learning and Developing

Adaptability and innovation are dynamic constructs. They aren't endpoint destinations where businesses arrive but are ongoing processes that necessitate continuous learning and development. By prioritizing ongoing learning programs and providing platforms for professional growth, employees can be better prepared to handle change, demonstrating more resilience and creativity.

3.4. Bridging the Gap with Cross-Functional Collaboration

Silos stifle adaptability. When different arms of a business function independently, their ability to respond to change collectively weakens. Fostering cross-functional collaboration can be instrumental in creating a culture of adaptability and innovation. This inter-departmental dialogue often brings to light new perspectives, ideas, and solutions that would have otherwise gone unnoticed.

3.5. Utilizing Technology to Foster Adaptability Mechanisms

In today's digital age, technology has a significant role to play in fostering a culture of adaptability. Whether it's the deployment of data analysis tools to unearth customer behavior patterns or the utilization of collaborative platforms that facilitate seamless communication, technology can provide the bedrock for adaptability strategies.

3.6. Leading by Example

Leadership plays a critical role in fostering a culture of adaptability and innovation. From openly embracing changes to showcasing an appetite for risk, the leadership's behavior creates a powerful precedent for the rest of the organization. Furthermore, leaders must be prepared to equitably allocate resources to innovative ventures, showing their commitment to the cause.

3.7. Measuring the Immeasurable

While adaptability and innovation might seem like abstract concepts, it's essential to develop concrete metrics for assessment. Whether it's gauging the frequency of new ideas, tracking the performance of new initiatives, or measuring the employees' readiness to embrace change, quantifying these elements brings transparency and accountability into the culture building process.

In conclusion, the process of fostering a culture of adaptability and innovation is neither swift nor easy; it requires time, detailed planning, and unwavering commitment from everyone in the organization. However, the impetus it can provide to a business's sustainability and growth in the ever-evolving market landscape makes this challenge undeniably worthwhile.

Chapter 4. Strategic Decision-Making for Sustainable Business Models

Strategic decision-making plays an undeniably pivotal role in molding sustainable business models. In an increasingly complex business landscape stamped by rapid change, enterprises must evolve their strategy-making apparatus beyond traditional confines and imbibe forward-thinking, resilient manners. Bearing this in mind, we elucidate an innovative, constituent-based approach to strategic decision-making, with sustainability at its core.

4.1. The Essence of Strategic Decision Making:

Every business decision, be it minor or major, directly influences the business's journey towards sustainability. Strategic decision-making is the process of making choices related to long-term, organization-wide strategies, intricately steered by top management. It sets the company's direction, impacting not only financial performance, but environmental and social footprints as well.

Decisions like entering new markets, developing new products, or changing supply chain practices carve strategic positions, thus shaping your business model's ability to sustain in the longer run. Hence, integrating sustainability into these choices is no longer a wishful luxury but a critical necessity.

4.2. Defining a Sustainable Business Model:

A sustainable business model is one where business success and sustainable practices walk hand-in-hand. It implies delivering superior value to all stakeholders – customers, employees, partners, ecosystems, and society at large, while minimizing negative environmental impacts. A sustainable model often involves innovation in business practices, partnerships, financing mechanisms, and customer relationships, propelling an enterprise's adaptability and long-term resilience.

4.3. Integrating Sustainability into Strategic Decision Making:

The key to inculcating sustainability into strategic decision-making lies in a systemic change in perspective. Traditional decision-making often revolves around immediate financial outcomes, but a sustainability-driven approach places equal emphasis on the long-run social and environmental implications.

1. **Identifying Strategic Decisions:** Begin by examining your corporate strategy to identify which decisions bear long-term implications. Common areas often include market choice, product development, sourcing procedures, and operational mechanisms.

2. **Understanding the Sustainability Landscape:** Build an understanding of sustainability-related trends, regulations, and practices within your industry and business context. By establishing a comprehensive view, you can cast forward-thinking strategies and avoid reactive adjustments.

3. **Stakeholder Engagement:** Actively involving stakeholders in your strategic decision-making process leads to a more holistic,

balanced strategy, incorporating multidimensional views and fostering increased commitment towards sustainability.

4. **Measurement and Reporting**: Measuring and transparently reporting sustainability impacts aids in presenting a clear picture of your sustainability strategy to stakeholders and facilitates subsequent improvements.

4.4. Leveraging Strategic Tools:

Utilizing deliberated strategic tools can augment the effectiveness of integrating sustainability into strategic decision-making. These include SWOT analysis, PESTLE analysis, Porter's Five Forces, scenario planning, and stakeholder mapping. These tools carve a more structured path for decision-making, enabling a deeper understanding of the market, competition, stakeholders, and trends.

4.5. Building Organizational Capacity:

For successful execution of sustainability-driven decisions, building organizational capacity is paramount. This underscores nurturing a sustainability-oriented culture, fostering employee engagement, instilling requisite skills, and employing technology for sustainable solutions.

4.6. The Role of Leadership:

Effective leadership plays a vital part in embedding sustainability into strategic decision-making. This necessitates leaders who not only articulate sustainability-driven vision and values but champion them through personal actions and company policies.

Strategic decision-making for sustainable business models is undeniably a Herculean task, more so in our contemporary VUCA world. Nonetheless, through thoughtful integration of sustainability into strategic decisions, a business can herald a transformation journey. It doesn't merely aid in building a resilient enterprise in the face of disruptions but steers the business towards developing a legacy of enduring growth and sustainability. Undoubtedly, these strategies form stepping stones to the unclaimed island – the treasure chest of opportunities, profitability, and long-term sustainability!

Chapter 5. Uncovering Emerging Market Opportunities

Understanding emerging markets and the opportunities they present is a significant step in future-proofing your business. With rapid digitalization, proliferation of technology and evolving consumer preferences, these markets are blooming with possibilities ripe for the taking. It requires discerning vision, strategic planning, and a practiced hand to navigate these dynamic terrains and capitalize on their prolific potential for growth.

5.1. The Potential of Emerging Markets

Emerging markets are often characterized by their fast-paced economic growth and development rates. They provide new consumer bases, increased demands for goods and services, and unique opportunities for partnerships and collaborations. However, their inherent volatility and potential governance challenges require a strategic, well-informed approach to capitalize on their growth potential.

Investing in emerging markets can significantly broaden a business's customer base, offering new demographics to market to and nurture. It can also lead to the discovery of novel product and service niches that have yet to be fully explored or capitalized upon. As globalization continues to blur geographical boundaries, it's more important than ever for businesses to look beyond their local markets and tap into the global economy's dynamism.

5.2. Identifying New Opportunities

Identifying new opportunities in these markets require a keen understanding of their unique socio-economic, cultural and political landscapes. Factors such as accelerated urbanization, expanding middle-class populations, improving literacy rates, and growing internet penetration contribute to the potential of these markets. It's essential to thoroughly research and analyze these trends to identify the most viable business opportunities.

Another critical element in opportunity identification is studying market competition. A comprehensive understanding of competitors can reveal gaps in the market. These gaps, whether in the product, service, or customer engagement, can be leveraged as opportunities for your business.

5.3. Leveraging Technology and Innovation

Technology plays an instrumental role in the success of a business in an emerging market. It aids in gaining a competitive edge through efficient processes, cost-reduction, and improving product and service quality. The latest advancements in AI, Machine Learning, IoT, Blockchain, go a long way in transforming business operations and customer experience in these markets. Embrace technology as a strategic tool for expansion and customer engagement rather than just an operational necessity.

Furthermore, innovation in business models and strategies can significantly drive market entry and success. Innovations should focus on localizing products or services to fit the market, integrating with local partners to extend market penetration, and devising creative engagement and marketing strategies to interact with consumers.

5.4. Building Local Partnerships

Local partnerships can expedite the market entry process and increase the overall success rate. Local partners can act as guides, helping you navigate the complex regulatory environment, understand the local business culture, and gain quicker market acceptance. They also bring numerous tangible and intangible benefits such as distribution networks, customer access, and market intelligence.

Building strategic alliances, franchising, and mergers and acquisitions can also be extremely beneficial. They can provide immediate access to resources, local knowledge, brands, and customers, paving the way for long-term business growth and expansion.

5.5. Managing Risks

While emerging markets offer tremendous opportunities, they also come with their share of risks. These entail, among others, political instability, currency fluctuations, and regulatory changes. A key to managing risk effectively is to constantly monitor the market and political situation, adapt to changes quickly, and diversify business investments across various markets to spread the risk.

A robust risk management strategy should be integrated into the overall business plan, where potential risks are identified, assessed, and mitigated. Investing in local professionals with deep market knowledge and understanding can help manage these risks effectively.

5.6. Conclusion: Embracing the Opportunities

Emerging markets abound with prospects for businesses willing to understand their unique dynamics, embrace their challenges, and venture into the unexplored territories. As we advance in this digital age, nascent markets are evolving faster than ever, offering opportunities for those ready to adapt and expand. By identifying these opportunities, leveraging technological advancements, building partnerships, and effectively managing risks, businesses can successfully navigate their path to a sustainable future in emerging markets.

Chapter 6. Technological Advancements and Their Role in Business Sustainability

Modern businesses cannot underestimate the power and potential of technological advancements. From streamlined operations to novel customer engagement methods, these advancements are redefining every aspect of running a business. However, the conversation around technology in business must now go beyond the simple question of efficiency and cost-effectiveness. It's time to delve into sustainability, an increasingly important aspect affecting every sector in today's world. In fact, technology's massive potential lies not just in bringing efficiencies but also in aiding the development of sustainable business models.

6.1. The Intersection of Technology and Sustainability

As global populations grow and resources continue to dwindle, businesses are starting to realize the importance of adopting sustainable practices. But how can businesses achieve this? The answer lies at the intersection of technology and sustainability. The technological advancements of the 21st century often align perfectly with an agenda for sustainability, providing businesses the tools they need to reduce their environmental impact and build more sustainable operations.

By applying these technological tools, businesses can increase their resource efficiency, reduce waste, and develop low-impact alternatives to traditional business processes. Artificial Intelligence

(AI), Big Data analytics, Internet of Things (IoT), and Blockchain are just a few examples of the technologies businesses can leverage. Not only can they help businesses become more sustainable, but they can also significantly improve their bottom line.

6.2. Harnessing the Power of Artificial Intelligence

AI, an offshoot of computer science that emphasizes the creation of intelligent machines that act and react like humans, has seen an explosive growth over the past few years. The sophisticated algorithms that drive AI can effectively analyze patterns and trends, to make businesses more efficient and reduce their environmental footprint.

For instance, consider Google's use of DeepMind AI to cut down its data center cooling costs by 40%, a significant reduction in energy usage and, therefore, environmental footprint. On a broader scale, AI can also allow businesses to streamline their supply chains, reduce waste, and design products that last longer and produce less waste.

6.3. Big Data Analytics

Big Data refers to the incredibly large datasets that pose challenges in processing using traditional methods. With advancements in processing power and analytic tools, we can now pull valuable insights from these datasets.

Businesses can harness the power of Big Data to improve sustainability in myriad ways. Energy usage, general waste, supply chain inefficiencies, and more can all be optimized by leveraging Big Data. A textbook example would be General Electric's use of Big Data in their wind turbine operations. By analyzing complex datasets, they were able to optimize turbine efficiency and reduce energy waste by a significant margin.

6.4. The Role of the Internet of Things

IoT is the concept of connecting any device to the Internet and to other connected devices. This interconnection provides us with valuable insights and control that we can use to optimize resources and reduce waste.

Whether it's energy-efficient smart buildings or sensor-laden industrial equipment that signal maintenance requirements before breakage occurs, thereby saving resources and reducing CO_2 emissions, IoT holds immense potential in driving sustainability in business operations.

6.5. Deciphering Blockchain for Sustainability

Historically associated with cryptocurrencies like Bitcoin, blockchain technology also has impressive sustainability applications. By enabling a transparent, tamper-proof record of transactions, blockchain can make supply chains more transparent, helping businesses eliminate waste and improve accountability.

Consumer goods giant, Unilever, for instance, used blockchain to track tea supply chains, promoting transparency and improving sustainability. Similarly, De Beers, the diamond corporation, uses blockchain to trace the origins of diamonds, supporting ethical and sustainable practices.

6.6. Building a Sustainable Future

While the tools are available, the transition towards a sustainable business model using technology is not without challenges. It requires a shift in business culture and values, fostering an environment where sustainability and profitability go hand in hand. And, this is not a one-man quest but a collective effort. It's about governments-making supportive policies, educational institutions-fostering research and development, investors-allocating funds wisely, and, most importantly, businesses-embracing technology for sustainable growth.

Technological advancements serve as a lighthouse showing businesses the path towards sustainable growth. Business-as-usual is no longer an option, and integrating sustainability into core business strategy using technology is both an imperative and an opportunity. For those who successfully navigate this change, the rewards are immense: efficiency, profitability, resilience, and the ultimate treasure – long-term business sustainability.

Chapter 7. Investing in People: Nurturing Talent for the Future

The lifeblood of any successful organization is its people. However, in today's rapidly changing technological landscape, the right skills and talents can become outdated with alarming speed. Investing in people not only refers to recruitment and retention but also nurtures talent for the future.

7.1. The Imperative of Talent Development

According to research by LinkedIn, 94% of employees would stay longer at a company that invested in their career development. This statistic underscores the essential role that people development plays in employee satisfaction, retention, and ultimately, business success.

Talent development, however, is not a once-off activity. It's an ongoing journey that helps individuals become better in existing roles, prepares them for future roles, and builds a versatile and agile talent pool suited to the changing business landscape.

7.2. Building a Culture of Learning

Developing talent begins with fostering a learning culture. This culture should be ingrained in the organization's DNA and reflected in its policies, procedures, and attitudes.

A learning culture encourages ongoing education, shared knowledge, and supports individual learning journeys. It values failure as a learning opportunity, promotes curiosity, and encourages challenging the status quo. In this culture, everyone, from entry-level employees to the C-suite, is dedicated to continuous learning and improvement.

Organizations can nurture a learning culture by providing learning resources, creating in-house learning opportunities, sponsoring external training, and encouraging staff to participate in learning activities.

7.3. Training and Upskilling

Preparing employees for tomorrow's jobs means charting an investment path today. It means identifying the future skills gaps and providing the necessary training and upskilling opportunities.

Investment in training and upskilling should be strategic and tailored to both the employee's current role and their career aspirations. These training programs should have clearly defined goals and outcomes, which are measurable and align with the business strategy.

One innovative strategy includes the creation of individualized "Learning Paths" for employees. However, it's essential to remember that one size doesn't fit all when it comes to talent development. Consideration should be given to different learning styles, career aspirations, and individual potential.

7.4. Fostering Knowledge Transfer and Cross-Functional Collaboration

Knowledge sharing and cross-functional collaboration are effective for breaking down silos, encouraging innovation, and preparing for future skills needs. Employees get the chance to understand the wider business, gain valuable experience, and develop their competencies.

Job shadowing, seconding employees to different departments, and collaborative projects are examples of practical ways to foster knowledge transfer and cross-functional collaboration.

7.5. Mentoring and Succession Planning

Mentoring programs not only guide less experienced employees but also prepare for future leadership roles. Furthermore, they reinforce the learning culture, encourage information sharing, and strengthen networks within the organization.

Succession planning should not be limited to leadership roles only, as critical skills can exist at all levels of the organization. Early identification of potential successors, coupled with targeted career development plans, can help businesses prepare for the future and mitigate the risks associated with key personnel's unexpected departure.

7.6. Measuring the Impact of Talent Development

Finally, to ensure these efforts are effective, companies must measure their impact. This can be achieved by tracking metrics such as increased job performance levels, reduced turnover rates, number of internal promotions, or improvements in overall business productivity and profitability.

In conclusion, investing in people is investing in the future of your business. By committing to ongoing talent development, fostering a learning culture, encouraging transfer of knowledge, and adopting a forward-thinking approach to succession planning, your organization can position itself at the forefront of change, underscore its attractiveness as an employer, and navigate the path to sustainable growth with confidence.

Chapter 8. Role of Social Responsibility in a Sustainable Business

The concept of social responsibility is evolving from a "nice to have" to a "business imperative". This significant shift is propelled by various factors including customer demands, investor pressures, and regulatory requirements. Specifically, customers are increasingly interested in supporting ethical businesses that have a positive impact on society and the environment while investors and regulators are demanding greater transparency concerning environmental, social, and governance (ESG) factors.

8.1. Understanding Social Responsibility

Social responsibility encapsulates the idea of businesses making decisions and taking actions that are in the best interest of society and the environment. This can involve a myriad of activities, from partnering with non-profit organizations to implementing environmentally friendly operations. It's not just about philanthropy, it's about deeply integrating these considerations into every aspect of their business model and recognizing the interdependencies between business success and societal well-being.

Social responsibility can be broken down into three predominant areas: environmental sustainability, corporate philanthropy, and ethical labor practices. Environmental sustainability pertains to a company's efforts to reduce its environmental footprint. Corporate philanthropy involves donating a portion of profits or resources to charitable causes. Ethical labor practices cover various practices ranging from fair wages and safe working conditions to diversity, inclusion, and equity.

8.2. Societal Expectations for Business

Society's expectations for businesses are on the rise. Consumers today expect businesses not just to provide quality products and services, but also to contribute positively to society. This is reflected in numerous studies showing that a considerable fraction of consumers are prepared to pay more for products from socially responsible companies.

Alongside consumer expectations, investor sentiment towards social responsibility is also shifting. More investors are applying ESG criteria in their investment decision-making processes and expecting companies to demonstrate their commitment to social responsibility.

Regulations too are catching up, with a growing number of governments around the world introducing regulations that urge or mandate companies to incorporate principles of social responsibility into their operations.

8.3. Integrating Social Responsibility into Your Business Strategy

Here are some steps businesses can take to integrate social responsibility into their business strategy.

1. Identify Social Responsibility Goals: Start by identifying what social responsibility means in the context of your business. This will involve looking at your business model and identifying areas where you can effect meaningful change. These goals should be

attainable, measurable, relevant, and aligned with your business' overall objectives.

2. Engage Stakeholders: Engage with your stakeholders, including employees, consumers, suppliers, investors, and the communities in which you operate. Their inputs can provide valuable insights that can help shape your social responsibility strategy.

3. Create a Strategic Plan: Once you've identified the areas of impact and engaged with your stakeholders, the next step is to develop a strategic plan. This plan will outline the steps you will take to achieve your social responsibility goals.

4. Implement the Strategy: With the strategic plan in place, the next phase is implementation. This may require changing current practices, training employees, or even overhauling your business model.

5. Monitor, Report and Improve: Once the strategy is implemented, it's crucial to monitor its effect and report these findings to stakeholders. These reports provide transparency and allow for continuous improvement.

8.4. The Business Case for Social Responsibility

Aside from fulfilling ethical obligations, there are tangible benefits to incorporating social responsibility into your business strategy. A commitment to social responsibility can lead to increased customer loyalty, attract top talent, increase employee morale, mitigate risks, attract investors, and potentially lead to cost savings - all of which contribute to long-term sustainability and profitability.

8.5. Conclusion

The role of social responsibility in a sustainable business can't be overstated. In today's business environment, it's not enough for companies to focus solely on achieving financial profit. Society expects businesses to also consider their environmental and social impact on the world. By integrating social responsibility into their business strategy, companies can not only meet these expectations but also unlock new opportunities for growth and value creation. Indeed, social responsibility is not just good for society, it's good for business too.

Chapter 9. Financing and Funding for a Sustainable Future

The need for adequate financing and funding to secure a sustainable future cannot be overstated. It plays a central role in not just sustaining operations, but also fueling innovation and managing risks.

9.1. Understanding Financing and Funding: The Green Perspective

Historically, financial and capital allocation was focused on short-term gains. But the trend today moves towards long-term, sustainable initiatives. The concept of "green financing" gained prominence to fund investments that ensure a positive environmental impact while providing economic prosperity.

Green financing can span across different areas such as renewable energy, resource conservation, biodiversity protection, and sustainable infrastructure. It encourages an integrated approach, where businesses, other than their usual operations, take initiatives to contribute to environmental sustainability.

9.2. Importance of Sustainable Investments

The importance of sustainable investments lies in its capacity to positively affect several areas of business. Fresh investment in sustainable projects facilitates job creation, contributes to a greener economy, and aids in combating climate change.

Furthermore, these investments often result in technological breakthroughs. Such developments might be related to green energy production, energy efficiency, or waste management, and they contribute towards the underlying goal of sustainability.

9.3. Vehicles for Green Financing

Green financing comes in many forms. Let's dive deeper into the specifics of some common vehicles of green financing.

9.3.1. Green Bonds

Green bonds serve as debt instruments issued by corporations, financial institutions, or governments to raise capital specifically for sustainable projects. The funds raised through these bonds are tightly linked to the achievement of environmentally friendly outcomes.

9.3.2. Green Funds

Green funds are mutual funds or exchange-traded funds that invest in companies focused on environmental sustainability. They offer a way for investors to contribute to green initiatives while participating in the financial returns that these companies generate.

9.3.3. Impact Investing

Impact investing refers to investments "made into companies, organizations, and funds with the intention to generate a measurable, beneficial social or environmental impact alongside a financial return".

9.4. Raising Capital for Sustainability: Points of Consideration

Raising capital for your green initiative can be a rewarding but challenging task. Here are some points to ponder:

9.4.1. Understanding Needs and Opportunities

Before seeking investment, you need to thoroughly understand the needs and opportunities of your initiative. Deconstruct your project into smaller units and assess the ways in which sustainable investment can facilitate your green plan.

9.4.2. Forming an Effective Proposal

Investors seek surety that their investment will convert into a profitable return, even in the case of green financing. An effective proposal emphasizes the potential of your sustainable projects in both environmental and financial contexts.

9.4.3. Leverage Government Policies

Governments often incentivize companies striving for sustainability. Whether it's tax breaks or grants, businesses should be adept at leveraging these incentives to complement their green initiatives.

9.5. Profiling Investors

It's crucial to understand your potential investor. Investors could range from government agencies, private equity firms, to individual social impact investors. Profiling them based on their past investments and interests will allow you to tailor a more compelling pitch.

9.6. Managing Risks

Adopting sustainable projects undoubtedly comes with risk. Yet, a solid risk management strategy can keep your initiative on track. Financial risks, regulatory risks, and environmental risks are some of the areas where sustainable businesses need to be vigilant.

In conclusion, sourcing financing and funding for a sustainable future requires a strategic approach. The process implies more than just sourcing funds—it's about developing a resilient, future-forward business. We invite you to embark on this journey of green financing for sustainable growth, navigating any obstacles that come your way using this comprehensive exploration as your guide. Both your business and our shared natural world will prosper in the long run.

Chapter 10. Managing Risks and Uncertainties Along the Path

In navigating the rugged landscape of an evolving business world, risk and uncertainty constitute challenging yet essential ingredients of the journey. Navigating through them requires a structured and progressive approach, underpinned by our views of uncertainty as a spectrum, not an absolute.

10.1. Understanding Risk and Uncertainty

Risk and uncertainty, while often used interchangeably, are distinct. Essentially, risk refers to situations where the outcomes are unknown but probabilities are known or can be estimated. Uncertainty, on the other hand, exists in situations where the outcomes and their probabilities are both unknown.

A proper understanding of these concepts forms the foundation upon which effective management strategies are built. Managing risks implies leveraging information and tools to estimate probabilities and outcomes to strategize accordingly. Managing uncertainty involves mitigating, adapting, or transforming behavior in response to unknown situations.

10.2. Incorporating Risk Management in Business Strategy

Risk management should not be a reactive band-aid solution, but a proactive, integral part of your strategic planning. Here's what comprises a comprehensive risk management strategy:

1. Identify and assess risks: Categorize them based on their potential impact and the likelihood of occurrence.

2. Develop strategies: Have strategies in place to deal with each risk category, considering the overall business objectives.

3. Implement and review: Execute the strategies and continually review their effectiveness.

Good risk management not only enables a business to navigate hurdles but also maximizes chances for success. One example is Google's Android platform. Recognizing the risk that Apple's iOS might dominate the market, Google identified a diversified strategy of offering a free, customizable mobile operating system to multiple manufacturers. This strategy effectively turned the tables and catapulted Android to its current market-leading position.

10.3. Integrating Uncertainty Management

Where risk management typically draws on 'hard' data, managing uncertainty requires a shift towards more intuitive and adaptive approaches.

1. Learning through experimentation: Operating in an uncertain environment is a process of learning. Quick, small-scale trials help assess what works and what doesn't.

2. Deepening market understanding: A nuanced insight into market trends, evolving customer needs, and the competitive landscape is invaluable.

3. Building resilience: Staying flexible and embracing agility enables businesses to pivot based on changed circumstances.

Companies like Netflix have shown how effective uncertainty

management can usher in industry transformations. Amid media industry uncertainties, Netflix invested heavily in creating and nurturing its streaming service to adapt to changing consumer behaviors and technological evolution.

10.4. Fostering a Culture of Resiliency

To minimize the detrimental impacts of risks and uncertainties, fostering a culture of resiliency is crucial. It empowers the organization to absorb shocks and bounce back stronger.

1. Promote agility: Encourage innovation and allow for flexibility in decision-making processes.

2. Create openness: Foster a culture of transparency where people can express concerns without fear.

3. Nurture collaboration: Enlist and fuse diverse ideas and abilities to create a robust shield against risks and uncertainties.

Amazon presents a prime example of resilience. The online retail giant faced significant risks and uncertainties in its early years, but its culture of being customer-obsessed, long-term oriented, and willing to be misunderstood allowed it to weather stormy phases and emerge prosperous.

10.5. Employing Technology for Risk and Uncertainty Management

Modern technological tools can aid in both risk and uncertainty management:

1. Big data and analytics: These can predict consumer behavior, identify potential threats, and pinpoint lucrative opportunities.

2. Machine Learning (ML) and Artificial Intelligence (AI): These tools can identify patterns and trends that may not be identifiable through human analysis.

3. Blockchain Technology: It can enhance the security, transparency, and traceability of transactions.

Dialog Semiconductor, a leading provider of battery and power management, utilized technological tools to manage the risk associated with reliance on Apple for 75% of its revenue. Leveraging predictive analytics, the company surfaced and understood this risk, enabling it to diversify its client base proactively.

10.6. Conclusion

The journey to a sustainable future doesn't promise to be risk-free or devoid of uncertainties, but knowing how to manage them can mark the difference between mere survival and success. Treat risks as calculations, uncertainties as gateways to innovation, and resilience as the hallmark of an adaptable enterprise.

Chapter 11. Transforming Challenges into Opportunities: Real-World Case Studies

Adaptability and flexibility form the robust backbone of any successful business. In this era of relentless disruption and volatility, the ability to turn challenges into opportunities not only ensures survival but also uncovers fresh avenues for exponential growth. For this analysis, we delve deep into the strategies adopted by remarkable organizations effectively navigating tough times, transforming challenges into gateways of opportunity.

11.1. Case Study 1: Blockbuster vs. Netflix

Perhaps one of the most infamous examples of a missed opportunity within the business world is that of Blockbuster, the physical movie rental store giant. This monolith, despite its dominant position, failed to adapt to online streaming, opening the door to a swift and ruthless takeover by Netflix. We can learn essential lessons from this highly evocative case.

In 2000, Reed Hastings, the co-founder of Netflix, allegedly proposed a partnership to Blockbuster. They dismissed the offer, underestimating the potential of online streaming and overestimating the longevity of their physical rental model. By the time Blockbuster noticed the shift in consumer behavior towards online consumption, Netflix had gained tremendous momentum. Netflix's forward-thinking innovation had basically created a new market, and they had first-mover advantage.

Blockbuster, trapped by its own inflexibility, ultimately filed for bankruptcy in 2010. In contrast, Netflix today has over 200 million subscribers worldwide, with a market cap of over $240 billion.

11.2. Case Study 2: Nokia vs. Apple

Another illuminating example of the importance of adaptation is Nokia, once the undisputed leader in the mobile phone industry. Nokia's focus on hardware, while crucial in the early days, became a hindrance as the industry started to see software and user interface as equally important.

Apple, conversely, recognized the impending shift and launched the iPhone, which transformed our conception of what a mobile phone could do. The iPhone was not just an elegant piece of hardware; it introduced a seamless user interface and a revolutionary ecosystem of apps, setting new standards that Nokia was unable to meet.

Despite having the resources, Nokia's rigidity in recognizing the importance of software led to a decline from which it has yet to recover. Nokia's market share dropped from 49.4% in 2007 to 3.1% in 2013, while Apple's increased from 2.7% to 15.2% in the same period.

11.3. Case Study 3: Kodak vs. Digital Photography

At the cusp of the digital revolution, Kodak dominated the photographic film market. They invented the digital camera in the mid-1970s but, ironically, anxious about cannibalizing their own film products, they underestimated their own invention's potential.

As digital photography gained traction, newer companies with more agile business models quickly moved in. By the time Kodak decided to transition to digital, it was too late. Their revenue dwindled, and they filed for bankruptcy in 2012.

On the other hand, companies like Canon and Sony were quick to adopt digital technology, resulting in tremendous growth in a much shorter time. They reaped the benefits of riding the wave of digital photography, capturing a substantial market share and creating a powerful brand image.

In conclusion, and as clearly evidenced, companies that demonstrate resilience and adaptability gain a competitive advantage. By focusing on optimizing their current operations while also investing in long-term change, businesses can better navigate global disruptions and eventualities. This approach lays the groundwork for sustainable success, underpinning the ultimate ability to transform challenges into opportunities.

Adapting to change always involves risk, but being risk-averse can turn out to be the greater hazard. History is strewn with examples of organizations that chose complacency over innovation, only to watch as more agile competitors claimed their share of the pie.

The principle remains constant: to secure a resilient and sustainable future, businesses must not only accept change but actively seek and embrace it. Always strive to exploit the new landscape that change presents: a fertile ground for new growth and uncharted opportunities. This is the true hallmark of successful, adaptable businesses; they leverage adversity as a catalyst for innovation and progress.